LIFE'S LITTLE
INSTRUCTION BOOK
Volume II

H. Jackson Brown, Jr.

Thorsons
An Imprint of HarperCollins*Publishers*

Thorsons
An Imprint of HarperCollins*Publishers*
77-85 Fulham Palace Road,
Hammersmith, London W6 8JB

Published by Thorsons 1993
First published in the USA by Rutledge Hill Press, Inc.,
211 Seventh Avenue North, Nashville, Tennessee 37219, 1993
1 3 5 7 9 10 8 6 4 2

© H. Jackson Brown, Jr. 1993

H. Jackson Brown, Jr. asserts the moral right to
be identified as the author of this work

A catalogue record for this book
is available from the British Library

ISBN 0 7225 2928 7

Printed in Great Britain by
HarperCollinsManufacturing Glasgow

INTRODUCTION

Life is a process. We are all works in progress – green tomatoes ripening on the windowsill of life. As I experience more, learn more, and contemplate more, I often think of what use my discoveries might be to my son, Adam.

Several years ago I jotted down a list of advice for him as he left home to begin college. At the time I thought the list was fairly complete.

But within a few days of presenting him with the 32 typed pages that became *Life's Little Instruction Book*, I began to think of other entries I wished I had included. How could I have forgotten to mention 'Never be the first to break a family tradition', or 'Believe in love at first sight', or practical advice like 'Don't ride a bicycle barefoot' and 'Never drive while holding a cup of coffee between your knees'? Obviously there was only one thing to do – start another list. I promised myself I wouldn't send it to him until it reached at least 512 entries – one more than the original list. It took two years to complete.

The day Adam received it, he called from his apartments. 'Dad,' he said, 'this new list is terrific. I think it's more useful than the first one. Does this mean I should look for a new volume of *Life's Little Instruction Book* every two years?'

'Would you like that?' I asked.

'Oh, yes,' he said.

'I'll see what I can do,' I replied, with not a small degree of satisfaction.

Little does Adam know that I can no more stop writing down these suggestions and observations than I could stop at a doughnut shop and order only coffee.

Life keeps coming at me, and new insights and discoveries get caught in my net. Like a fisherman, I haul them up, sort the catch, and head for the harbour. It's late and getting dark. But up ahead, standing on the dock, is a young man holding a lantern welcoming me. It's my son, Adam.

Also by H. Jackson Brown

LIFE'S LITTLE INSTRUCTION BOOK

512 ♦ Believe in love at first sight.

513 ♦ Never laugh at anyone's dreams.

514 ♦ Overpay good baby sitters.

515 ♦ Love deeply and passionately. You might get hurt, but it's the only way to live life completely.

516 ◆ Accept a breath mint if someone offers you one.

517 ◆ Take along a small gift for the host or hostess when you're a dinner guest. A book is a good choice.

518 ◆ Discipline with a gentle hand.

519 ◆ Talk slowly
but think quickly.

520 ◆ Open the car door for your wife and always help her with her coat.

521 ◆ If called for jury service, look on it positively. You'll learn a lot.

522 ◆ When reconvening after a conference break, choose a chair in a different part of the room.

523 ♦ Read the books shortlisted each year for the Booker Prize.

524 ♦ Rake a big pile of leaves every autumn and jump in it with someone you love.

525 ♦ Volunteer. Sometimes the jobs no one wants conceal big opportunities.

526 ◆ Never drive while holding a cup of hot coffee between your knees.

527 ◆ Carry a container of wet wipes in your glove compartment.

528 ◆ Park in the end space in car parks. Your car doors will have half the chance of getting dented.

529 ◆ To dry wet shoes, stuff them with newspaper and let them dry naturally.

530 ◆ Never miss an opportunity to ride a roller coaster.

531 ◆ Don't let your family get so busy that you don't sit down to at least one meal a day together.

532 ◆ Never miss an opportunity to sleep outside in hot weather.

533 ◆ Sign all guarantee cards and send them in promptly.

534 ◆ Drive as you wish your kids would. Never speed or drive recklessly with children in the car.

535 ◆ Ask about a shop's return policy when you purchase an item that costs more than £50.

536 ◆ Never be the first to break a family tradition.

537 ◆ Never miss an opportunity to have someone rub your back.

538 ◆ Keep a diary of your accomplishments at work. Then when you ask for a raise, you'll have the information you need to back it up.

539 ◆ Have a professional photo of yourself made. Update it every three years.

540 ◆ Don't judge people by their relatives.

541 ◆ In disagreements, fight fairly. No name calling.

542 ◆ Use a travel agent. It costs no more and saves time and effort.

543 ◆ Remember that everyone you meet is afraid of something, loves something, and has lost something.

544 ◆ When you go to borrow money, dress as if you have plenty of it.

545 ◆ Never take the last piece of fried chicken.

546 ◆ Check hotel bills carefully, especially the charges for local and long-distance calls.

547 ◆ Eat a piece of chocolate to cure bad breath from onions or garlic.

548 ◆ Never sign contracts with blank spaces.

549 ◆ Remember the three Rs: Respect for self; Respect for others; Responsibility for all your actions.

550 ◆ Put your address inside your luggage as well as on the outside.

551 ◆ Don't admire people for their wealth but for the creative and generous ways they put it to use.

552 ◆ Never pick up anything off the floor of a cab.

553 ♦ Seize every opportunity for additional training in your job.

554 ♦ When travelling, leave the good jewellery at home.

555 ♦ Take along two big safety pins when you travel so that you can pin the curtains shut in your hotel room.

556 ◆ When someone asks you a question you don't want to answer, smile and ask, 'Why do you want to know?'

557 ◆ Never give your credit card number over the phone unless you made the call and are sure who you are speaking to.

558 ◆ Remember that just the moment you say, 'I give up,' someone else seeing the same situation is saying, 'My, what a great opportunity.'

559 ◆ Never betray a confidence.

560 ◆ Never leave the kitchen when something's boiling on the stove.

561 ♦ Never claim a victory prematurely.

562 ♦ Say 'bless you' when you hear someone sneeze.

563 ♦ Make the punishment fit the crime.

564 ♦ Keep the porch light on until all the family is in for the night.

565 ◆ Remember that everyone is influenced by kindness.

566 ◆ Never give anybody a fondue set or anything painted avocado green.

567 ◆ Carry your own alarm clock when travelling. Hotel wake-up calls are sometimes unreliable.

568 ♦ Pack a compass and a Swiss Army knife when hiking in unfamiliar territory.

569 ♦ Never apologize for being early for an appointment.

570 ♦ Plant courgettes only if you have lots of friends.

571 ◆ Borrow a box of puppies for an afternoon and take them to visit the residents of a retirement home. Stand back and watch the smiles.

572 ◆ When you lose, don't lose the lesson.

573 ◆ When you feel terrific, notify your face.

574 ♦ Don't be surprised to discover that luck favours those who are prepared.

575 ♦ When lost or in distress, signal in 'threes' – three shouts, three gunshots, or three horn blasts.

576 ♦ Never be photographed with a cocktail glass in your hand.

577 ◆ Don't let a little dispute injure a great friendship.

578 ◆ Don't marry anyone who picks at their food.

579 ◆ When asked to play the piano, do it without complaining or making excuses.

580 ◆ Create a little signal only your wife knows so that you can show her you love her across a crowded room.

581 ◆ Read a book about beekeeping.

582 ◆ Subscribe to *Which?* magazine.

583 ◆ Carry a small pocket knife.

584 ◆ Keep a well-stocked first-aid kit in your car and at home.

585 ◆ Order a seed catalogue. Read it the day after the clocks go back.

586 ◆ Every so often, invite the person behind you in the queue to go ahead of you.

587 ◆ Don't overlook life's small joys while searching for the big ones.

588 ◆ Look for ways to make your boss look good.

589 ◆ When you have the choice of two exciting things, choose the one you haven't tried.

590 ♦ Take off the conference badge as soon as you leave the venue.

591 ♦ Remember that the person who steals an egg will steal a chicken.

592 ♦ Meet regularly with someone who holds vastly different views from you.

593 ◆ Give people more
than they expect
and do it cheerfully.

594 ◆ Remember that no time spent with your children is ever wasted.

595 ◆ Don't go looking for trouble.

596 ◆ Don't buy someone else's trouble.

597 ◆ Don't expect your love alone to make a neat person out of a messy one.

598 ◆ Be the first to fight for a just cause.

599 ◆ Remember that no time is ever wasted that makes two people better friends.

600 ◆ Check to see if your own car insurance covers you when you rent a car. The insurance offered by car rental companies is expensive.

601 ◆ There are people who will always come up with reasons why you can't do what you want to do. Ignore them.

602 ◆ Avoid approaching horses and restaurants from the rear.

603 ◆ Never say anything uncomplimentary about another person's dog.

604 ◆ If you need to bring in a business partner, make sure your partner brings along some money.

605 ◆ Never miss a chance to dance with your wife.

606 ◆ Don't ride in a car if the driver has been drinking.

607 ◆ If you have trouble with a company's products or services, go to the top. Write to the managing director, then follow up with a phone call.

608 ◆ Think twice before accepting the lowest bid.

609 ◆ Don't judge what you don't understand.

610 ◆ Pay your bills on time. If you can't, write your creditors a letter describing your situation. Send them something every month, even if it's only five pounds.

611 ◆ When boarding a bus, say 'hello' to the driver. Say 'thank you' when you get off.

612 ♦ When uncertain what to wear, a blue blazer, worn with grey wool slacks, a white shirt, and a red-and-blue striped silk tie, is almost always appropriate.

613 ♦ When in doubt about what art to put on a wall, choose a framed black-and-white photo by Ansel Adams.

614 ◆ Never give a gift that's not beautifully wrapped.

615 ◆ When you realize you've made a mistake, take immediate steps to correct it.

616 ◆ Don't think expensive equipment will make up for lack of talent or practice.

617 ◆ Learn to say 'I love you' in French, Italian and Swedish.

618 ◆ Own an umbrella big enough for two people to share without getting wet.

619 ◆ Make allowances for your friends' imperfections as readily as you do for your own.

620 ◆ Don't waste time trying to appreciate
music you dislike. Spend the time
with music you love.

621 ◆ When you are totally exhausted but
have to keep going, wash your face
and hands and put on clean socks
and a clean shirt. You will feel
remarkably refreshed.

622 ◆ Write a short note inside the front cover when giving a book as a gift.

623 ◆ When concluding a business deal and the other person suggests working out the details later, say, 'I understand, but I would like to settle the entire matter right now.' Don't move from the table until you do.

624 ♦ Make the rules for your children clear, fair and consistent.

625 ♦ Be ruthlessly realistic when it comes to your finances.

626 ♦ Do your homework and know your facts, but remember it's passion that persuades.

627 ◆ Set high goals for your employees and help them attain them.

628 ◆ Set aside your dreams for your children and help them attain their own dreams.

629 ◆ Smile when picking up the phone. The caller will hear it in your voice.

630 ♦ Ask anyone giving you directions to repeat them at least twice.

631 ♦ Steer clear of any place with a 'Ladies Welcome' sign in the window.

632 ♦ Be open and accessible. The next person you meet could become your best friend.

633 ◆ Always put something
in the collection plate.

634 ◆ Ask yourself if you would feel comfortable giving your two best friends a key to your house. If not, look for some new best friends.

635 ◆ Do the right thing, regardless of what others think.

636 ◆ Buy the big bottle of Tabasco.

637 ◆ Judge people from where they stand,
not from where you stand.

638 ◆ When shaking a woman's hand,
squeeze it no harder than she
squeezes yours.

639 ◆ Never wash a car, mow a lawn, or
select a Christmas tree after dark.

640 ◆ Life will sometimes hand you a magical moment. Savour it.

641 ◆ Don't give away the ending of good films and books.

642 ◆ Learn to save on even the most modest salary. If you do, you're almost assured of financial success.

643 ♦ Dress a little better than your clients but not as well as your boss.

644 ♦ Take the stairs when it's four flights or less.

645 ♦ Buy a used car with the same caution a naked man uses to climb a barbed-wire fence.

646 ◆ Memorize your favourite love poem.

647 ◆ Never threaten if you don't intend to back it up.

648 ◆ Hold yourself to the highest standards.

649 ◆ Be the first to forgive.

650 ♦ Don't confuse comfort with happiness.

651 ♦ Don't confuse wealth with success.

652 ♦ Wear smart clothes to job interviews, even for a job stacking shelves.

653 ♦ Don't cut corners.

654 ◆ Whenever you take something back for an exchange or refund, wear a jacket and tie.

655 ◆ Check for toilet paper *before* sitting down.

656 ◆ Every year celebrate the day you and your partner had your first date.

657 ◆ Don't knock the competition.

658 ◆ Make a habit of reading something inspiring and cheerful just before going to sleep.

659 ◆ Marry someone you love to talk to. As you get older, conversational skills will be as important as any other.

660 ◆ If you work for an organization that makes its decisions by committee, make sure you're on the committee.

661 ◆ When employing people, give special consideration to anyone who's gained a Duke of Edinburgh's Award.

662 ◆ Spend some time alone.

663 ◆ Never buy anything electrical at a market.

664 ◆ Remember that a person who is foolish with money is foolish in other ways too.

665 ◆ Everyone loves praise. Look hard for ways to give it to them.

666 ◆ When talking to your doctor, don't let him or her interrupt or end the session early. It's your body. Stay until all your questions are answered to your satisfaction.

667 ◆ Everyone deserves a birthday cake. Never celebrate a birthday without one.

668 ♦ If you want to do something and you feel in your bones that it's the right thing to do, do it. Intuition is often as important as the facts.

669 ♦ Be as friendly to the security guard as you are to the chairman of the board.

670 ♦ Learn to bake bread.

671 ◆ When it comes to worrying or painting a picture, know when to stop.

672 ◆ Before taking a long trip, fill your tank and empty your bladder.

673 ◆ Open your arms to change, but don't let go of your values.

674 ♦ Be an original. If that means being a little eccentric, so be it.

675 ♦ Pay as much attention to the things that are working positively in your life as you do to those that are giving you trouble.

676 ♦ Give a poor child an Easter egg.

677 ♦ Ask for double prints when you have film processed. Send the extras to the people in the photos.

678 ♦ Treat your employees with the same respect you give your clients.

679 ♦ Slow down. I mean *really* slow down when there's a school nearby.

680 ♦ Turn enemies into friends by doing something nice for them.

681 ◆ When taking a woman home, make sure she's safely inside her house before you leave.

682 ◆ You may be fortunate and make a lot of money. But be sure your work involves something that enriches your spirit as well as your bank account.

683 ♦ Allow your children to face the consequences of their actions.

684 ♦ Conduct yourself in such a way that your old school would want you to make a speech at Prizegiving.

685 ♦ Don't expect the best gifts to come wrapped in pretty paper.

686 ◆ Live with your new pet several days before you name it. The right name will come to you.

687 ◆ When a good man or woman runs for political office, support him or her with your time and money.

688 ◆ What you must do, do cheerfully.

689 ◆ Remember that silence is sometimes the best answer.

690 ◆ Don't dismiss a good idea simply because you don't like the source.

691 ◆ Don't think you can relax your way to happiness. Happiness comes as a result of *doing*.

692 ♦ Don't buy a cheap mattress.

693 ♦ Don't expect anyone to know what you want for Christmas if you don't tell them.

694 ♦ Don't waste time waiting for inspiration. Begin, and inspiration will find you.

695 ◆ When you need professional advice, get it from professionals, not from your friends.

696 ◆ Choose a church that sings joyful music.

697 ◆ Don't believe all you hear, spend all you have, or sleep all you want.

698 ◆ Win without boasting.

699 ◆ Lose without excuses.

700 ◆ Watch your attitude. It's the first thing people notice about you.

701 ◆ Be engaged at least six months before you get married.

702 • Be quick to take advantage of an advantage.

703 ◆ When you say, 'I love you,' mean it.

704 ◆ When you say, 'I'm sorry,' look the person in the eye.

705 ◆ Pack a light bathrobe on overnight trips. Take your pillow, too.

706 ◆ Choose the top floor flat.

707 ♦ Ask someone you'd like to know better to list five people he would most like to meet. It will tell you a lot about him.

708 ♦ Don't be a person who says, 'Ready, fire, aim.'

709 ♦ Don't be a person who says, 'Ready, aim, aim, aim.'

710 ◆ Deadlines are important. Meet them.

711 ◆ When you find someone doing small things well, put him or her in charge of bigger things.

712 ◆ Remove your sunglasses when you talk to someone.

713 ◆ Watch less TV.

714 ◆ Remember that a good price is not necessarily what an object is marked, but what it is worth to you.

715 ◆ When a friend or loved one becomes ill, remember that hope and positive thinking are strong medicines.

716 ◆ Remember that the more you know, the less you fear.

717 ◆ When a waitress or waiter provides exceptional service, leave a generous tip, plus a short note like, 'Thanks for the wonderful service.'

718 ◆ Read more books.

719 ◆ Buy three best-selling children's books. Read them and then give them to a youngster.

720 ◆ Introduce yourself to your neighbours as soon as you move into a new area.

721 ◆ Be your children's best teacher and coach.

722 • When opportunity knocks, invite it to stay for dinner.

723 ◆ When you find something you really want, don't let a few pounds keep you from getting it.

724 ◆ Don't confuse mere inconveniences with real problems.

725 ◆ Strive for perfection, but settle for excellence.

726 ♦ Some things need doing better than they've ever been done before. Some just need doing. Others don't need doing at all. Know which is which.

727 ♦ When travelling by plane, don't pack valuables or important papers in your suitcase. Carry them on board with you.

728 ♦ Show extra respect for people whose jobs put dirt under their fingernails.

729 ♦ Don't do business with anyone who has a history of suing people.

730 ♦ Hold your child's hand as often as you can. The time will come all too soon when he or she won't let you.

731 ♦ When you carve the Christmas turkey, give the first piece to the person who prepared it.

732 ♦ Live a good, honourable life. Then when you get older and think back, you'll enjoy it a second time.

733 ♦ Learn to juggle.

734 ♦ Purchase one piece of original art each year, even if it's just a small oil painting by a student.

735 ♦ Volunteer to help a few hours a month working in a soup kitchen.

736 ♦ Wipe the sticky honey jar before putting it back on the shelf.

737 ◆ Don't think people at the top of their professions have all the answers. They don't.

738 ◆ Learn to make great spaghetti sauce.

739 ◆ If you're treated unfairly by an airline, contact the Air Transport Users' Committee on 071-242 3882.

740 ◆ Get a car with a sun roof.

741 ◆ Don't carry expensive luggage. It's a tip off to thieves that expensive items may be inside.

742 ◆ Buy ladders, extension cords and garden hoses longer than you think you'll need.

743 ◆ Be humble and polite, but don't let anyone push you around.

744 ◆ Put your jacket around your girlfriend on a chilly evening.

745 ◆ Once every couple of months enjoy a four-course meal – but eat each course at a different restaurant.

746 ◆ Introduce yourself to someone you
would like to meet by smiling
and saying, 'My name is Adam
Brown. I haven't had the pleasure
of meeting you.'

747 ◆ Be advised that when negotiating,
if you don't get it in writing, you
probably won't get it.

748 ♦ Wrap a couple of thick rubber bands around your wallet when you're fishing or hiking. This will prevent it from slipping out of your pocket.

749 ♦ Do 100 push-ups every day: 50 in the morning and 50 in the evening.

750 ♦ Keep your private thoughts private.

751 ◆ Put the strap around your neck before looking through binoculars.

752 ◆ Don't expect bankers to come you your aid in a crisis.

753 ◆ Every so often let your spirit of adventure triumph over your good sense.

754 ◆ Remember that
a good example is the
best sermon.

755 ♦ Wear goggles when operating a power saw or drill.

756 ♦ Use a favourite picture of a loved one as a bookmark.

757 ♦ Before going to bed on Christmas Eve, join hands with your family and sing 'Silent Night'.

758 ♦ Surprise an old friend with a phone call.

759 ♦ Get involved at your child's school.

760 ♦ Champion your spouse. Be his or her best friend and biggest fan.

761 ♦ Don't accept unacceptable behaviour.

762 ◆ Carry a list of your spouse's important measurements in your wallet.

763 ◆ Add to your children's private library by giving them a hardback copy of one of the classics every birthday. Begin with their first birthday.

764 ◆ Read between the lines.

765 ♦ Don't say no until you've heard the whole story.

766 ♦ When you are a dinner guest, take a second helping if it's offered, but never a third.

767 ♦ Write your favourite author a note of appreciation.

768 ◆ Never lose your nerve, your temper, or your car keys.

769 ◆ Don't open credit card bills at the weekend.

770 ◆ Never start the car until all passengers have fastened their seat belts.

771 ◆ Never say anything uncomplimentary about your wife or children in the presence of others.

772 ◆ Send you mother-in-law flowers on your wife's birthday.

773 ◆ Use your past successes as a trampoline, not as an easy chair.

774 ◆ When eating at a restaurant that features foreign food, don't order anything you could make at home.

775 ◆ Apologize immediately when you lose your temper, especially to children.

776 ◆ Buy your fiancée the nicest diamond engagement ring you can afford.

777 ◆ When you're uncertain of what you should pay someone, ask, 'What do you think is fair?' You'll almost always get a reasonable answer.

778 ◆ Be wary of the man who's 'all hat and no cattle'.

779 ◆ Read Thoreau's *Walden*.

780 • Trust in God
but lock your car.

781 ◆ When giving a speech, concentrate on what you can give the audience, not what you can get from them.

782 ◆ Don't be so concerned with your rights that you forget your manners.

783 ◆ Remember that almost everything looks better after a good night's sleep.

784 ◆ A loving atmosphere in your home is so important. Do all you can to create a tranquil, harmonious home.

785 ◆ Use a camcorder to videotape the contents of your home for insurance purposes. Don't forget cupboards and drawers. Keep the tape in your bank safe-deposit box.

786 ♦ When you know that someone has gone to a lot of trouble to get dressed up, tell them they look terrific!

787 ♦ Avoid using the word *impacted* unless you are describing wisdom teeth.

788 ♦ Keep a separate shaving kit packed for travelling.

789 ◆ Stop and watch a farmer ploughing a field.

790 ◆ When you tell a child to do something, don't follow it with, 'Okay?' Ask instead, 'Do you understand?'

791 ◆ Spend a day at the races.

792 ♦ When you see visitors taking pictures of each other, offer to take a picture of their group together.

793 ♦ Mind the store. No one cares about your business the way you do.

794 ♦ Get to car boot sales early. The good stuff is usually gone by 8.00 A.M.

795 ◆ Stop and watch stonemasons at work.

796 ◆ Choose a subject you know nothing about and start trying to learn all you can about it.

797 ◆ In disagreements with loved ones, deal with the current situation. Don't bring up the past.

798 ◆ Every so often watch *Blue Peter*.

799 ◆ Remember that *how* you say something is as important as *what* you say.

800 ◆ Never apologize for extreme measures when defending your values, your health or your family's safety.

801 • Don't let weeds grow
around your dreams.

802 ♦ Don't think you can fill an emptiness in your heart with money.

803 ♦ Become famous for finishing important, difficult tasks.

804 ♦ Never sell your teddy bear, school scarf or favourite childhood books. You'll regret it later.

805 ♦ Leave a small coin where a child can find it.

806 ♦ Clean out a different drawer in your house every week.

807 ♦ Do a good job because you want to, not because you have to. This puts you in charge instead of your boss.

808 ♦ Buy a new tie to wear to your wedding. Wear it only once. Keep it forever.

809 ♦ When you're lost, admit it, and ask for directions.

810 ♦ Never type a love letter. Use a fountain pen.

811 ◆ Place a note reading 'Your licence number has been reported to the police' on the windshield of a car illegally parked in a disabled space.

812 ◆ Remember that the shortest way to get anywhere is to have good company travelling with you.

813 ◆ Never buy just one roll of toilet paper, one roll of film or one jar of peanut butter. Get two.

814 ◆ Never buy a chair or sofa without first sitting on it for several minutes.

815 ◆ At the end of your days, be leaning forward – not falling backwards.

816 ♦ Don't be thin-skinned. Take criticism as well as praise with equal grace.

817 ♦ Never eat liver at a restaurant. Some things should be done only in the privacy of one's home.

818 ♦ Share your knowledge. It's a way to achieve immortality.

819 ◆ Don't take good friends, good health or a good marriage for granted.

820 ◆ Keep impeccable tax records.

821 ◆ Help a child plant a small garden.

822 ◆ Don't work for a company let by someone of questionable character.

823 ◆ Spend your time and energy creating, not criticising.

824 ♦ Read bulletin boards at the supermarket, college bookshop and launderette. You will find all sorts of interesting things there.

825 ♦ The next time you meet a police officer, firefighter or ambulance worker, tell them that you appreciate what they do.

826 ◆ Act with courtesy and fairness regardless of how others treat you. Don't let them determine your response.

827 ◆ When working with contractors, include a penalty clause in your contract for their not finishing on time.

828 ♦ Visit your old school and introduce yourself to the head. Ask if you can sit in on a couple of classes.

829 ♦ Respect sailing boats, snowmobiles and motorcycles. They can teach you a painful lesson very fast

830 ♦ Challenge yourself. Aim high.

831 ◆ In a verbal confrontation, lower your
voice to the degree that the other
person raises his or hers.

832 ◆ Let your children see you do things
for your wife that lets them know
how much you love and treasure her.

833 ◆ Don't leave hair in the shower drain.

834 ◆ Learn three knock-knock jokes so you will always be ready to entertain children.

835 ◆ When you are a dinner guest at a restaurant, don't order anything more expensive than your host does.

836 ◆ Don't outlive your money.

837 ♦ Take photographs of every car you own. Later, these photos will trigger wonderful memories.

838 ♦ Remember that nothing really important ever happens until someone takes a chance.

839 ♦ Never grab at a falling knife.

840 ◆ Think twice before deciding not to charge for your work. People often don't value what they don't pay for.

841 ◆ When someone offers to pay you now or later, choose now.

842 ◆ Don't take nine items to the eight items or less queue.

843 ♦ Never take what you can't use.

844 ♦ When there is a hill to climb, don't think that waiting will make it smaller.

845 ♦ When your dog dies, frame its collar and put it above a window facing west.

846 ♦ When a garment label warns 'Dry Clean Only', believe it.

847 ♦ Beware the life empty of ambitions.

848 ♦ Write the date and the names of non-family members on the backs of all photos as soon as you get them back from the developer.

849 • Be gentle
with the Earth.

850 ◆ Read a lot when you're on vacation, but nothing that has to do with your business.

851 ◆ Start every day with the most important thing you have to do. Save the less important tasks for later.

852 ◆ Mind your own business.

853 ◆ At meetings, resist turning around to see who has just arrived late.

854 ◆ Don't ride a bicycle or motorcycle barefooted.

855 ◆ Refuse to share personal and financial information unless you feel it is absolutely essential.

856 ◆ Just because you earn a decent wage, don't look down on those who don't. To put things in perspective, consider what would happen to the public good if you didn't do your job for 30 days. Next, consider the consequences if sanitation workers didn't do their jobs for 30 days. Now, whose job is more important?

857 ◆ Don't purchase anything in a package that appears to have been opened.

858 ◆ Be willing to lower your price in order to get something else of greater value.

859 ◆ Remember that what's right isn't always popular, and what's popular isn't always right.

860 ◆ Pray. There is immeasurable power in it.

861 ◆ Call a nursing home or retirement centre and ask for a list of the residents who seldom get mail or visitors. Send them a card several times a year. Sign it, 'Someone who thinks you are very special'.

862 ◆ Schedule your stag night at least two days before your wedding.

863 ◆ Before buying a house or renting a flat, check the water pressure by turning on the taps and the shower and then flushing the toilet.

864 ◆ Don't do business with people who knock on your door and say, 'I just happened to be in the neighbourhood.'

865 ◆ Properly fitting shoes should feel good as soon as you try them on. Don't believe the salesperson who says, 'They'll be fine as soon as you break them in.'

866 ◆ When making toast, don't put the knife back in the butter after you've put it in the marmalade.

867 ◆ Overestimate travel time by 15 per cent.

868 ◆ Choose a business partner the way you choose a tennis partner. Select someone who's strong where you are weak.

869 ◆ Make duplicates of all important keys.

870 ◆ Get your hair cut a week before the big interview.

871 ◆ Spend your life lifting people up, not putting them down.

872 ◆ Don't trust a woman or man who doesn't close their eyes when you kiss them.

873 ◆ Never interrupt when you are being flattered.

874 ◆ Never tell a person who's experiencing deep sorrow, 'I know how you feel.' You don't.

875 ◆ In business or in life, don't follow the wagon tracks too closely.

876 ◆ Own a comfortable chair for reading.

877 ◆ Own a set of good kitchen knives.

878 ◆ Own a stylish hat.

879 ◆ Don't call a fishing rod a 'pole', a line a 'rope', a rifle a 'gun' or a ship a 'boat'.

880 ◆ Brush your teeth before putting on your tie.

881 ◆ Never risk what you can't afford to lose.

882 ◆ Keep candles and matches in the kitchen and bedroom in case of power failure.

883 • Remember that great love and great achievements involve great risk.

884 ♦ Never tell a man he's losing his hair. He already knows.

885 ♦ Learn to use a needle and thread, a steam iron, and an espresso machine.

886 ♦ Display your street number prominently on your house in case emergency vehicles need to find you.

887 ◆ Never say, 'My child would never do that.'

888 ◆ Once a year, go somewhere you've never been before.

889 ◆ Remember that what you give will afford you more pleasure than what you get.

890 ◆ For peace of mind, make decisions in concert with your values.

891 ◆ Remember that ignorance is expensive.

892 ◆ If you make a lot of money, put it to use helping others while you are living. That is wealth's greatest satisfaction.

893 ◆ Get your name off mailing lists by writing to: Mailing Preference Service, Freepost 22, London W1E 7EZ, with your name, address and postcode.

894 ◆ Listen to your critics. They will keep you focused and innovative.

895 ◆ Never say anything to a news reporter that you don't want to see on the front page of your local paper. Comments made 'off the record' seldom are.

896 ◆ Remember that not getting what you want is sometimes a stroke of good luck.

897 ◆ Don't pick up after your children,
That's their job.

898 ◆ Remember the old proverb, 'Out of
debt, out of danger'.

899 ◆ When someone has provided you
with exceptional service, write a note
to his or her boss.

900 ◆ When declaring your rights, don't forget your responsibilities.

901 ◆ Replace the batteries in smoke alarms every January 1st.

902 ◆ Never ask an accountant, lawyer or doctor professional questions in a social setting.

903 ♦ Perform your job better than anyone else can. That's the best job security.

904 ♦ Remember that everyone you meet wears an invisible sign. It reads 'Notice me. Make me feel important.'

905 ♦ Never employ someone you wouldn't invite home to dinner.

906 ◆ Think twice before accepting a job that requires you to work in an office with no windows.

907 ◆ When camping or hiking, never leave evidence that you were there.

908 ◆ Dress respectfully when attending church.

909 ◆ Remember that your child's character is like good soup. Both are homemade.

910 ◆ Don't allow your dog to bark and disturb the neighbours.

911 ◆ For easier reading in hotel rooms, pack your own 100-watt lightbulb.

912 ◆ If you've learned that a good friend is ill, don't ask him about it. Let him tell you first.

913 ◆ If you lend someone money, make sure his character exceeds the collateral.

914 ◆ Go to air displays.

915 ◆ Be cautious telling people how contented and happy you are. Many will resent it.

916 ◆ Hang up if someone puts you on hold to take a 'call waiting'.

917 ◆ Put love notes in your child's lunch box.

918 ♦ Every once in a while ask yourself that question, If money weren't a consideration, what would I like to be doing?

919 ♦ Remember that the best relationship is one where your love for each other is greater that your need for each other.

920 • Learn the rules.
Then break some.

921 ♦ Remember that half the joy of achievement is in the anticipation.

922 ♦ Accept the fact that regardless of how many times you are right, you will sometimes be wrong.

923 ♦ Whether it's life or a horse that throws you, get right back on.

924 ◆ No matter how old you get, hug and kiss your mother whenever you greet her.

925 ◆ Encourage anyone who is trying to improve mentally, physically or spiritually.

926 ◆ Go to charity cricket matches.

927 ♦ Go to barbecues.

928 ♦ Order a charity Christmas catalogue.

929 ♦ Keep in touch with your childhood friends – you have a lot of shared past.

930 ♦ Help your children set up their own savings accounts by the age of 16.

931 ◆ Get involved with your local government. As someone said, 'Politics is too important to be left to the politicians.'

932 ◆ When trying on new clothes, take your wallet with you when you leave the changing room to look in the mirror.

933 ♦ Never swap your integrity for money, power or fame.

934 ♦ Never tell an off-colour joke when people of a different generation are present.

935 ♦ Learn to play 'Happy Birthday' on the piano.

936 ◆ Never sell yourself short.

937 ◆ Never remind someone of a kindness
or act of generosity you have shown
him or her. Bestow a favour and then
forget it.

938 ◆ Put on old clothes before you get out
the paint brushes.

939 ◆ Fool someone on April 1st.

940 ◆ When you need assistance, ask this way: 'I've got a problem. I wonder if you would be kind enough to help me?'

941 ◆ When you get really angry, stick your hands in your pockets.

942 ◆ Never be ashamed of honest tears.

943 ◆ Never be ashamed of laughter that's too loud or singing that's too joyful.

944 ◆ Never be ashamed of your patriotism.

945 ◆ Don't trust your memory; write it down.

946 ◆ Always try the house salad dressing.

947 ◆ If your child's teacher is particularly good, tell the head.

948 ◆ At least once, date someone with beautiful red hair.

949 ◆ Watch the film *Regarding Henry*.

950 ◆ Watch the film *Mr Smith Goes to Washington*.

951 ◆ Visit friends and relatives when they are in hospital. You only need to stay a few minutes.

952 ◆ Never leave a youngster in the car without taking the car keys.

953 ◆ Don't think that sending a gift or flowers substitutes for your presence.

954 ◆ When visiting a small town at lunch time, choose the café on the square.

955 ◆ Attach a small Christmas wreath to your car's grill on the first day of December.

956 ◆ Never ask a barber if you need a haircut.

957 ◆ Truth is serious business. When criticizing others, remember that a little goes a long way.

958 ◆ Don't confuse foolishness with bravery.

959 ♦ When your children are learning to play musical instruments, buy them good ones.

960 ♦ Don't discuss domestic problems at work.

961 ♦ Never 'borrow' so much as a pencil from your workplace.

962 • Judge your success by what you had to give up in order to get it.

963 ◆ Never buy a piece of jewellery that costs more than £100 without doing a little haggling.

964 ◆ Travel. See new places, but remember to take along an open mind.

965 ◆ Be especially courteous and patient with older people.

966 ◆ Become a tourist for a day in your own home town. Take a tour. See the sights.

967 ◆ A racehorse that consistently runs just a second faster than another horse is worth millions of dollars more. Be willing to give that extra effort that separates the winner from the one in second place.

968 ◆ Create a smoke-free office and home.

969 ◆ Never eat a sugared doughnut when wearing a dark suit.

970 ◆ Remember this statement by Coach Lou Holtz, 'Life is 10 per cent what happens to me and 90 per cent how I react to it.'

971 ♦ Answer the easy questions first.

972 ♦ Never ignore evil.

973 ♦ Don't mistake kindness for weakness.

974 ♦ Never get a tattoo.

975 ♦ Let some things remain mysterious.

976 ♦ Call before dropping in on friends and family.

977 ♦ When you are away from home and hear church bells, think of someone who loves you.

978 ♦ Every now and then, bite off more than you can chew.

979 ◆ Never decide to do nothing just because you can only do a little. Do what you can.

980 ◆ Acknowledge a gift, no matter how small.

981 ◆ Remember that your character is your destiny.

982 ◆ Let your handshake be as binding as a signed contract.

983 ◆ Keep and file the best business letters you receive.

984 ◆ Grind it out. Hanging on just one second longer than your competition makes you the winner.

985 ◆ Buy and use your customers' products.

986 ◆ Be better prepared than you think
you will need to be.

987 ◆ Buy a small, inexpensive camera.
Take it with you everywhere.

988 ◆ When friends offer to help, let them.

989 • Approach love and cooking with reckless abandon.

990 ◆ Pay the extra £5 for the best seats at a play or concert.

991 ◆ Buy a red umbrella. It's easier to find among all the black ones, and it adds a little colour to rainy days.

992 ◆ Employ people more for their judgement than for their talents.

993 ◆ Every week, write a short poem.

994 ◆ Worry makes for a hard pillow. When something's troubling you, before going to sleep, jot down three things you can do the next day to help solve the problem.

995 ◆ Love someone who doesn't deserve it.

996 ◆ Never buy anything from a rude salesperson, no matter how much you want it.

997 ◆ Give handout materials after your presentation, never before.

998 ◆ Every so often, go where you can hear seagulls crying.

999 ♦ When you mean no, say it in a way that's not ambiguous.

1000 ♦ Attend a local fair or gala and support your community.

1001 ♦ When you're buying something that you only need to buy once, buy the best you can afford.

1002 ◆ Never open a restaurant.

1003 ◆ Give children toys that are powered by their imagination, not by batteries.

1004 ◆ Choose a seat in the row next to the emergency exit when flying. You will get more leg room.

1005 ♦ Reject and condemn prejudice based on race, gender, religion or age.

1006 ♦ As soon as you get married, start saving for your children's education.

1007 ♦ Read a magazine every week that has nothing to do with your hobbies or work.

1008 ♦ You may dress unconventionally, but remember that the more strangely you dress, the better you have to be.

1009 ♦ Be suspicious of a boss who schedules meetings instead of making decisions.

1010 ♦ Carry three business cards in your wallet.

1011 ◆ Life is short.
Eat more pancakes and
fewer rice cakes.

1012 ◆ Give the price of a night out to Shelter.

1013 ◆ Don't overfeed horses or brothers-in-law.

1014 ◆ For emergencies, always have a 50 pence piece in your pocket and a five pound note hidden in your wallet.

1015 ◆ Regardless of the situation, react with class.

1016 ◆ Buy raffle tickets, sweets and baked goods from pupils who are raising money for school projects.

1017 ◆ Become the kind of person who brightens a room just by entering it.

1018 ♦ Remember the observation of William James that the deepest principle in human nature is the craving to be appreciated.

1019 ♦ When there's a piano to be moved, don't reach for the stool.

1020 ♦ Root for the home team.

1021 ♦ Go on blind dates. Remember, that's how I met your mother.

1022 ♦ Someone will always be looking at you as an example of how to behave. Don't let them down.

1023 ♦ Remember that the 'suggested retail price' seldom is.

1024 ◆ Follow your own star.

1025 ◆ Remember the ones who love you.

1026 ◆ Go home for the holidays.

1027 ◆ Don't get too big for your boots.

1028 ◆ Call your dad.

Dear Reader,

If you received advice from your parents or grandparents that was especially meaningful and you would like me to share it with other readers, please write and tell me about it.

I look forward to hearing from you.

H. Jackson Brown, Jr.
c/o Thorsons
77-85 Fulham Palace Road
Hammersmith
LONDON W6 8JB

God's Little
Instruction Book
on Success

HONOR
BOOKS

Tulsa, Oklahoma

God's Little Instruction Book on Success
ISBN 1-56292-084-7
Copyright © 1996 by Honor Books, Inc.
P. O. Box 55388
Tulsa, Oklahoma 74155

Manuscript prepared by W. B. Freeman Concepts, Inc., Tulsa, Oklahoma

Introduction

Many people would define success as fame, fortune, or a good reputation. Some may even extend the definition to include integrity of character and acts of giving. However, the achievement of all these qualities can still leave one with a sense of emptiness.

The Bible's description of a successful person is someone who has established an intimate relationship with the Heavenly Father, desiring to please Him in all areas of their life. Such a life of faith in God brings forth these qualities of success a deep sense of fulfillment, lasting joy, and inner peace.

In the words of an anonymous writer, "Success is an *inside* story" — one that begins in the heart and radiates outwardly.

To Laugh Much And Often;
To Win the Respect Of Intelligent People
And The Affection Of Little Children;
To Earn The Appreciation Of Honest Critics
And Endure the Betrayal Of False Friends;
To Appreciate Beauty, To Find The Best In Others;
To Leave The World A Bit Better,
Whether By a Healthy Child, A Garden Patch
Or a Redeemed Social Condition;
To Know Even One Life Has Breathed Easier
Because You Lived.
This Is to Have Succeeded.

— Ralph Waldo Emerson

Blessed (happy, fortunate, prosperous, and enviable) is the man who walks and lives not in the counsel of the ungodly [following their advice, their plans and purposes]...But his delight and desire are in the law of the Lord, and on His law (the precepts, the instructions, the teachings of God) he habitually meditates (ponders and studies) by day and by night....and everything he does shall prosper [and come to maturity].

Psalm 1:1-3 AMP

Success in the world means power, influence, money, prestige. But in the Christian world, it means pleasing God.

And whatever we ask we receive from Him, because we keep His commandments and do those things that are pleasing in His sight.
1 John 3:22 NKJV

Success isn't measured by the position you reach in life; it's measured by the obstacles you overcome.

Blessed is the man who perseveres under trial, because when he has stood the test, he will receive the crown of life that God has promised to those who love him.
James 1:12

Effort is supreme joy. Success is not a goal, but a means to aim still higher.

I know that I have not yet reached that goal, but there is one thing I always do ...I keep trying to reach the goal and get the prize for which God called me through Christ to the life above.
Philippians 3:13-14
NCV

Success is 10 percent inspiration and 90 percent perspiration.

The plans of the dilegent lead to profit as surely as haste leads to poverty.
Proverbs 21:5

9

We can do anything we want to do if we stick to it long enough.

You need endurance, so that when you have done the will of God, you may receive what was promised.
Hebrews 10:36
NRSV

A diamond is a piece of coal that stuck to its job.

When he has tested me, I shall come out like gold. My foot has held fast to his steps.
Job 23:10-11
NRSV

11

Failure isn't so bad if it doesn't attack the heart. Success is all right if it doesn't go to the head.

A man's pride will bring him low, but the humble in spirit will retain honor.
Proverbs 29:23
NKJV

He who would climb the ladder must begin at the bottom.

Anyone wanting to be a leader among you must be your servant. And if you want to be right at the top, you must serve like a slave.
Matthew 20:26-27 TLB

Step by step,
little by little, bit by bit
— that is the way to wealth,
that is the way to wisdom,
that is the way to glory.

Precept upon precept, rule upon rule,...here a little, there a little...the Lord will teach.
Isaiah 28:10-11
AMP

14

How can they say my life is not a success? Have I not for more than sixty years got enough to eat and escaped being eaten?

For we brought nothing into this world, and it is certain we can carry nothing out. And having food and raiment let us be therewith content.
1 Timothy 6:7-8
KJV

15

The dictionary is the only place that success comes before work. Hard work is the price we must pay for success.

Lazy hands make a man poor, but diligent hands bring wealth.
Proverbs 10:4

Have a purpose in life, and having it, throw into your work such strength of mind and muscle as God has given you.

Live purposefully and worthily and accurately, not as the unwise and witless, but as wise (sensible, intelligent people), making the very most of the time [buying up each opportunity]. Ephesians 5:15-16 AMP

17

When success turns a man's head, he faces failure.

Talk no more so very proudly, let not arrogance come from your mouth; for the Lord is a God of knowledge, and by him actions are weighed.
1 Samuel 2:3
NRSV

The first step on the way to victory is to recognize the enemy.

Discipline yourselves, keep alert. Like a roaring lion your adversary the devil prowls around, looking for someone to devour. Resist him, steadfast in your faith.
1 Peter 5:8-9
NRSV

Everybody finds out, sooner or later, that all success worth having is founded on Christian rules of conduct.

Glory and honor and peace to every man who does good.
Romans 2:10
NASB

By success, of course, I do not mean that you may become rich, famous, or powerful...I mean the development of mature and constructive personality.

Perseverance must finish its work so that you may be mature and complete, not lacking anything.
James 1:4

Success depends on backbone, not wishbone.

Then you will have success if you are careful to observe the decrees and laws that the Lord gave Moses for Israel. Be strong and courageous. Do not be afraid or discouraged.
1 Chronicles 22:13

Half the failures in life arise from pulling in one's horse as he is leaping.

Jesus replied, "No one who puts his hand to the plow and looks back is fit for service in the kingdom of God."
Luke 9:62

Success in life is a matter not so much of talent or opportunity as of concentration and perseverance.

Let us not get tired of doing what is right, for after a while we will reap a harvest of blessing if we don't get discouraged and give up.
Galatians 6:9 TLB

There is a close correlation between getting up in the morning and getting up in the world.

A little sleep, a little slumber, a little folding of the hands to rest — and poverty will come on you like a bandit and scarcity like an armed man.
Proverbs 6:10,11

≈

I make progress by having people around me who are smarter than I am — and listening to them.

Let the wise also hear and gain in learning.
Proverbs 1:5 NRSV

Success is being able to come home, lay your head on the pillow and sleep in peace.

His peace will keep your thoughts and your hearts quiet and at rest as you trust in Christ Jesus.
Philippians 4:7
TLB

~

You've got to continue to grow, or you're just like last night's cornbread — stale and dry.

Be careful so you will not fall from your strong faith. But grow in the grace and knowledge of our Lord and Savior Jesus Christ.
2 Peter 3:17-18
NCV

I t's not enough to get all the breaks. You've got to know how to use them.

He who gathers crops in summer is a wise son, but he who sleeps during harvest is a disgraceful son.
Proverbs 10:5

Success that is easy is cheap.

He is a rewarder of those who diligently seek Him.
Hebrews 11:6
NKJV

A purpose is the eternal condition of success.

Where there is
no vision, the
people perish.
Proverbs 29:18
KJV

Ninety-nine percent of failures come from people who have the habit of making excuses.

But they all alike began to make excuses.... I tell you, not one of those men who were invited will get a taste of my banquet.
Luke 14:18,24

There is in this world no such force as the force of a man determined to rise.

Let us lay aside every weight, and the sin which so easily ensnares us, and let us run with endurance the race that is set before us.
Hebrews 12:1
NKJV

To have grown wise and kind is real success.

Therefore, as God's chosen, set apart and enjoying His love, clothe yourselves with tenderness of heart, kindliness, humility, gentleness, patient endurance.
Colossians 3:12
MLB

Three qualities vital to success: toil, solitude, prayer.

Do not let this Book of the Law depart from your mouth; meditate on it day and night, so that you may be careful to do everything written in it. Then you will be prosperous and successful.
Joshua 1:8

35

There is not a man that has not "his hour," and there is not a thing that has not its place.

There is an appointed time for everything. And there is a time for every event under heaven.
Ecclesiastes 3:1
NASB

Success is more a function of consistent common sense than it is of genius.

Commit your work to the Lord, then it will succeed.
Proverbs 16:3 TLB
~

When you make a mistake, admit it; learn from it and don't repeat it.

Godly sorrow brings repentance that leads to salvation and leaves no regret.
2 Corinthians 7:10

Success won at the cost of self-respect is not success.

For what will a man be profited, if he gains the whole world, and forfeits his soul?
Matthew 16:26
NASB

One important key to success is self-confidence. An important key to self-confidence is preparation.

Study to show thyself approved unto God, a workman that needeth not to be ashamed, rightly dividing the word of truth.
2 Timothy 2:15
KJV

4

Six essential qualities that are the key to success: sincerity, personal integrity, humility, courtesy, wisdom, charity.

Do your best to improve your faith. You can do this by adding goodness, understanding, self-control, patience, devotion to God, concern for others, and love.... If you keep on doing this, you won't stumble and fall.
2 Peter 1:5-7,10
CEV

41

The simple virtues of willingness, readiness, alertness, and courtesy will carry a young man farther than mere smartness.

The people blessed all the men who willingly offered themselves.
Nehemiah 11:2
NKJV

In my vocabulary, there is no such word as "can't," because I recognize that my abilities are given to me by God to do what needs to be done.

I can do everything God asks me to with the help of Christ who gives me the strength and power.
Philippians 4:13
TLB
≈

The man who works for the gold in the job rather than for the money in the pay envelope is the fellow who gets on.

In all the work you are doing, work the best you can. Work as if you were doing it for the Lord, not for people.
Colossians 3:23
NCV

The man who will use his skill and constructive imagination to see how much he can give for a dollar, instead of how little he can give for a dollar, is bound to succeed.

By your standard of measure, it shall be measured to you.
Matthew 7:2
NASB

The smile of God
is victory.

*Do what is right
and good in
the sight of
the Lord.
Deuteronomy
6:18 NKJV*

'Tis man's to fight,
but Heaven's
to give success.

*The Lord says,
"Don't be afraid!
Don't be
paralyzed by this
mighty army! For
the battle is not
yours, but God's!"
2 Chronicles
20:15 TLB*

To be a winner in life, we must first be a winner inside.

It is sheer waste of time... to imagine what I would do if things were different. They are not different.

Brothers, I do not consider myself yet to have taken hold of it. But one thing I do: Forgetting what is behind and straining toward what is ahead.
Philippians 3:13

≈

49

The surest way not to fail is to determine to succeed.

Choose for yourselves this day whom you will serve.
Joshua 24:15
NKJV

The only thing that stops you is yourself. Period.

Create in me a pure heart, O God, and renew a steadfast spirit within me.
Psalm 51:10

The young man who would succeed must identify his interests with those of his employer and exercise the same diligence in matters entrusted to him as he would in his own affairs.

And if ye have not been faithful in that which is another man's, who shall give you that which is your own?
Luke 16:12 KJV

~

It is the amount and excellence of what is over and above the required that determines the greatness of ultimate distinction.

Having confidence in your obedience, I write to you, knowing that you will do even more than I say.
Philemon 1:21
NKJV

To become an able and successful man in any profession, three things are necessary: nature, study, and practice.

Be a good workman, one who does not need to be ashamed when God examines your work. Know what his Word says and means.
2 Timothy 2:15
TLB

If you wish success in life, make *perseverance* your bosom friend, *experience* your wise counselor, *caution* your elder brother, and *hope* your guardian genius.

Knowing that tribulation brings about perseverance; and perseverance, proven character; and proven character, hope; and hope does not disappoint.
Romans 5:3-5
NASB

The worst bankrupt in the world is the man who has lost his enthusiasm. Let a man lose everything else in the world but his enthusiasm and he will come through again to success.

It is fine to be zealous, provided the purpose is good, and to be so always.
Galatians 4:18

D o not attempt to do a thing unless you are sure of yourself; but do not relinquish it simply because someone else is not sure of you.

In quietness and confidence shall be your strength.
Isaiah 30:15 NKJV

The worst use that can be made of success is to boast of it.

As has been written, "Let the boaster boast in the Lord."
1 Corinthians 1:31 MLB

Aim at perfection in every thing, though in most things it is unattainable; however, they who aim at it, and persevere, will come much nearer to it, than those whose laziness and despondency make them give it up as unattainable.

You are to be perfect, even as your Father in heaven is perfect.
Matthew 5:48 TLB

Never one thing and seldom one person can make for a success. It takes a number of them merging into one perfect whole.

Under his direction the whole body is fitted together perfectly, and each part in its own special way helps the other parts, so that the whole body is healthy and growing and full of love.
Ephesians 4:16
TLB

Snowflakes are one of nature's most fragile things, but just look what they can do when they stick together.

Let us not give up meeting together, as some are in the habit of doing, but let us encourage one another.
Hebrews 10:25

~

Behind every successful man there's a lot of unsuccessful years.

He lifted me out of the slimy pit, out of the mud and mire; he set my feet on a rock and gave me a firm place to stand.
Psalm 40:2

Success generally depends upon knowing how long it takes to succeed.

Perseverance must finish its work so that you may be mature and complete, not lacking anything.
James 1:4

~

63

No man will succeed unless he is ready to face and overcome difficulties and prepared to assume responsibilities.

If you want to build a tower, you first sit down and decide how much it will cost, to see if you have enough money to finish the job.
Luke 14:28 NCV

Many people have the ambition to succeed; they may even have special aptitude for their job. And yet they do not move ahead. Why? Perhaps they think that since they can master the job, there is no need to master themselves.

He that hath no rule over his own spirit is like a city that is broken down, and without walls.
Proverbs 25:28
KJV

The recipe for successful achievement:
1. Enjoy your work.
2. Do your best.
3. Develop good working relationships.
4. Be open to opportunities.

Blessed is the man who listens to me, watching daily at my gates, waiting at my doorposts, for he who finds me finds life, and obtains favor from the Lord.
Proverbs 8:34-35
NASB

A long time ago a noted specialist said that his secret of success as a physician was keeping the patient's head cool and his feet warm. And it is just now becoming generally known that a "hot head" and "cold feet" are enough to bring disaster to even a well man.

He who is slow to anger is better than the mighty. And he who rules his spirit than he who takes a city.
Proverbs 16:32
NKJV

No wind blows in favor of a ship without a destination.

I press toward the goal for the prize of the upward call of God in Christ Jesus.
Philippians 3:14
NKJV

I f you don't like the road you're walking, start paving another one.

Rise up; this matter is in your hands. We will support you, so take courage and do it.
Ezra 10:4

Less is more is true
not only in writing,
but in life.

*Even a fool is
thought wise if he
keeps silent, and
discerning if he
holds his tongue.*
Proverbs 17:28

Success for the striver washes away the effort of striving.

They that sow in tears shall reap in joy.
Psalm 126:5 KJV

There is nothing like a fixed, steady aim, with an honorable purpose. It dignifies your nature, and insures your success.

Therefore do not be foolish, but understand what the Lord's will is.
Ephesians 5:17

If you have a good name...if you can face your God and say, "I have done my best," then you are a success.

A good name is rather to be chosen than great riches, and loving favour rather than silver and gold.
Proverbs 22:1 KJV

~

He that would have fruit must climb the tree.

Put in the sickle for the harvest is ripe.
Joel 3:13 NASB

~

The gent who wakes up and finds himself a success hasn't been asleep.

Whatever your hand finds to do, do it with all your might.
Ecclesiastes 9:10

75

The necessary ingredients for enjoying success:

1. Simple tastes
2. A certain degree of courage
3. Self-denial to a point
4. Love of work
5. A clear conscience

We are confident that we have a good conscience, in all things desiring to live honorably.
Hebrews 13:18
NKJV

~

The most important single ingredient in the formula of success is knowing how to get along with people.

In humility consider others better than yourselves. Each of you should look not only to your own interests, but also to the interests of others.
Philippians 2:3-4

L asting success rarely comes to those who do not first decide to succeed.

He knows enough to refuse evil and choose good.
Isaiah 7:15 NASB

We would accomplish many more things if we did not think of them as impossible.

The things impossible with men are possible with God.
Luke 18:27 NASB

79

I have made mistakes, but I have never made the mistake of claiming that I never made one.

Confess your faults one to another, and pray one for another, that ye may be healed.
James 5:16 KJV
~

Success is never final and failure never fatal. It's courage that counts.

So we say with confidence, "The Lord is my helper, I will not be afraid. What can man do to me?"
Hebrews 13:6

~

F ailure is the halfway
mark on the road
to success.

*For he has
delivered me from
all my troubles,
and my eyes have
looked in triumph
on my foes.
Psalms 54:7*

Failure is often that early morning hour of darkness which precedes the dawning of the day of success.

In the world ye shall have tribulation: but be of good cheer; I have overcome the world.
John 16:33 KJV

~

I couldn't wait for success ...so I went ahead without it.

So David triumphed over the Philistine with a sling and a stone; without a sword in his hand he struck down the Philistine and killed him.
1 Samuel 17:50

Success requires the vision to see, the faith to believe, and the courage to do.

Be on your guard; stand firm in the faith; be men of courage; be strong.
1 Corinthians 16:13

There are no shortcuts to any place worth going.

The gate is small and the road is narrow that leads to true life.
Matthew 7:14
NCV

~

Don't wait for your ship to come in; swim out to it.

I am the Lord, who opens a way through the waters, making a path right through the sea.
Isaiah 43:16 TLB

Every man should make up his mind that if he expects to succeed, he must give an honest return for the other man's dollar.

But as for me, I walk in my integrity.
Psalm 26:11 NRSV

~

Character is the real foundation of all worthwhile success.

Walk in the way of goodness, and keep to the paths of righteousness. For the upright will dwell in the land.
Proverbs 2:20-21
NKJV

It takes twenty years to make an overnight success.

Diligent hands will rule, but laziness ends in slave labor.
Proverbs 12:24

To climb steep hills
Requires slow pace
at first.

Though your beginning was small, yet your latter end would greatly increase.
Job 8:7 AMP

Always aim for achievement and forget about success.

So we make it our goal to please him.
2 Corinthians 5:9

To follow, without halt, one aim: There's the secret of success.

But Jesus told him, "Anyone who lets himself be distracted from the work I plan for him is not fit for the Kingdom of God."
Luke 9:62 TLB

93

The world is not interested in the storms you encountered, but did you bring in the ship?

[Jesus] got up, rebuked the wind and said to the waves, "Quiet! Be still!" Then the wind died down and it was completely calm. He who believes in Me, the works that I do shall he do also.
Mark 4:39 NIV,
John 14:12 NASB

The measure of success is not whether you have a tough problem to deal with, but whether it's the same problem you had last year.

But the God of all grace, who hath called us unto his eternal glory by Christ Jesus, after that ye have suffered a while, make you perfect, stablish, strengthen, settle you.
1 Peter 5:10 KJV

The strength of a man consists in finding out the way God is going, and going that way.

My soul shall be joyful in the Lord; it shall rejoice in His salvation.
Psalm 35:9 NKJV

Four steps to achievement: plan purposefully, prepare prayerfully, proceed positively, pursue persistently.

Now all the work of Solomon was well-ordered from the day of the foundation of the house of the Lord until it was finished. So the house of the Lord was completed.
2 Chronicles 8:16
NKJV

T he secret of all victory lies in the organization of the non-obvious.

But God hath chosen the foolish things of the world to confound the wise; and God hath chosen the weak things of the world to confound the things which are mighty.
1 Corinthians
1:27 KJV

Success in life comes not from holding a good hand, but in playing a poor hand well.

To him who overcomes, I will grant to eat of the tree of life.
Revelation 2:7
NASB

The talent of success is nothing more than doing what you can do well; and doing well whatever you do, without a thought of fame.

But remember the Lord your God, for it is he who gives you power to get wealth, so that he may confirm his covenant that he swore to your ancestors.
Deuteronomy 8:18 NRSV

A winner is someone who recognizes his God-given talents, works his tail off to develop them into skills, and uses these skills to accomplish his goals.

The man who had received the five talents brought the other five. "Master," he said, "you entrusted me with five talents. See, I have gained five more." Matthew 25:20

~

There is no limit to the good a man can do if he doesn't care who gets the credit.

"My food," said Jesus, "is to do the will of him who sent me and to finish his work."
John 4:34

There is no substitute for hard work.

He who cultivates his land will have plenty of bread, but he who follows worthless people and pursuits will have poverty enough.
Proverbs 28:19
AMP

If you succeed in all you do, it's a sure sign you're not reaching high enough.

Seek those things which are above.
Colossians 3:1
NKJV

Those who aim low usually hit their targets.

For as he thinketh in his heart, so is he.
Proverbs 23:7
KJV

Do in life what you would do even if no one paid you for it — do what you are passionate about. Soon men will pay almost anything for your services.

Do you see a man skilled in his work? He will serve before kings; he will not serve before obscure men.
Proverbs 22:29

~

The successful person is the individual who forms the habit of doing what the failing person doesn't like to do.

Go watch the ants, you lazy person. Watch what they do and be wise.
Proverbs 6:6 NCV

You have to experience failure in order to understand success.

If you do what the Lord wants, he will make certain each step you take is sure. The Lord will hold your hand, and if you stumble, you still won't fall.
Psalm 37:23-24
CEV

A wise man will make more opportunity than he finds.

A man's gift maketh room for him, and bringeth him before great men.
Proverbs 18:16
KJV

A failure is a man who has blundered, but is not able to cash in on the experience.

Correct those with understanding, and they will gain knowledge.
Proverbs 19:25
NCV

M

ore people talk themselves into failure than talk themselves into success.

Your words now reflect your fate then: either you will be justified by them or you will be condemned.
Matthew 12:37
TLB

111

Don't aim for success if you want it; just do what you love and believe in, and it will come naturally.

Take delight in the Lord, and he will give you the desires of your heart.
Psalm 37:4 NRSV

Happiness, wealth, and success are by-products...they should not be the goal.

Seek first His kingdom and His righteousness; and all these things shall be added to you.
Matthew 6:33
NASB

～

113

Determine that the thing can and shall be done, and then we shall find the way.

Is anything too difficult for the Lord? Genesis 18:14 NASB

11

Confidence of success ...often induces real success.

Being confident of this very thing, that he which hath begun a good work in you will perform it until the day of Jesus Christ.
Philippians 1:6
KJV

115

Falling in love with one's job is the secret of success.

He who finds his life will lose it, and he who loses his life for My sake will find it.
Matthew 10:39
NKJV

~

116

Success lies in this: Do your best. Then expect God's best.

All these blessings shall come upon you and overtake you, because you obey the voice of the Lord your God. Deuteronomy 28:2 NKJV

The only people who achieve much are those who want knowledge so badly that they seek it while the conditions are still unfavorable.

As the deer pants for the water brooks, so pants my soul for You, O God.
Psalm 42:1 NKJV

Y ou have to want it [success] bad. You can find geniuses on any skid row and average intellects as presidents of banks. It's what pushes you from inside.

Do you not know that in a race all the runners run, but only one gets the prize? Run in such a way as to get the prize.
1 Corinthians 9:24
≈

L et me tell you the secret that has led me to my goal. My strength lies solely in my tenacity.

When Gideon came to the Jordan, he and the three hundred men who were with him crossed over, exhausted but still in pursuit.
Judges 8:4 NKJV

~

On the clarity of your ideas depends the scope of your success in any endeavor.

So I turned my mind to understand, to investigate and to search out wisdom and the scheme of things and to understand the stupidity of wickedness and the madness of folly.
Ecclesiastes 7:25

The road to success is dotted with many tempting parking places.

We want each of you to show this same diligence to the very end, in order to make your hope sure.
Hebrews 6:11

Success results as much from what we don't choose to do as it does from what we choose to do.

I have set before you life or death, blessing or curse. Oh, that you would choose life.
Deuteronomy 30:19 TLB

123

Success consists of getting up more times than you fall.

Though a righteous man falls seven times, he rises again.
Proverbs 24:16

One of the most important lessons of life is that success must continually be won and is never finally achieved.

For everyone who keeps on asking receives; and he who keeps on seeking finds; and to him who keeps on knocking, [the door] will be opened.
Matthew 7:8 AMP

125

You may have to fight a battle more than once to win it.

Hold on to what you have, so that no one will take your crown.
Revelation 3:11

⁓

D iligence is the mother of good fortune.

The plans of the diligent lead surely to advantage, but everyone who is hasty comes surely to poverty.
Proverbs 21:5
NASB

Success in life depends upon the three I's: integrity, intelligence, and industry.

Keep a clear conscience so that those who speak evil of your good life in Christ will be made ashamed.
1 Peter 3:16 NCV

Success is peace of mind, which is a direct result of knowing you did your best to become the best that you are capable of becoming.

Do not conform any longer to the pattern of this world, but be transformed by the renewing of your mind. Then you will be able to test and approve what God's will is — his good, pleasing and perfect will. Romans 12:2

The secret of success is to be like a duck — smooth and unruffled on the top, but paddling furiously underneath.

Better a patient man than a warrior, a man who controls his temper than one who takes a city.
Proverbs 16:32

If A is success in life, then A equals x plus y plus z. Work is x, y is play, and z is keeping your mouth shut.

Those who are careful about what they say keep themselves out of trouble.
Proverbs 21:23
NCV

131

A great secret of success is to go through life as a man who never gets used up.

But they that wait upon the Lord shall renew their strength; they shall mount up with wings as eagles; they shall run, and not be weary; and they shall walk, and not faint.
Isaiah 40:31 KJV

1

Success is not the result of spontaneous combustion. You must set yourself on fire.

For this reason I remind you to fan into flame the gift of God.
2 Timothy 1:6

The difference between failure and success is doing a thing nearly right and doing it exactly right.

The wicked man does deceptive work, but he who sows righteousness will have a sure reward.
Proverbs 11:18
NKJV

Make yourself indispensable and you'll be moved up. Act as if you're indispensable and you'll be moved out.

Solomon, seeing that the young man was industrious, made him the officer over all the labor force of the house of Joseph.
1 Kings 11:28
NKJV

135

I have never believed that any success outside the home can compensate for failure within it.

Blessed is the man who fears the Lord, who finds great delight in his commands. His children will be mighty in the land.
Psalm 112:1-2

~

13

If you want to learn about success, listen to someone who has succeeded.

Hear, O sons, the instruction of a father, and give attention that you may gain understanding, for I give you sound teaching.
Proverbs 4:1-2
NASB

Before everything else, getting ready is the secret of success.

Suppose one of you wants to build a tower. Will he not first sit down and estimate the cost to see if he has enough money to complete it?
Luke 14:28

Success is achieving the goals you have set for yourself.

But the noble man devises noble plans; and by noble plans he stands.
Isaiah 32:8 NASB

139

I cannot give you the formula for success but I can give you the formula for failure — which is: Try to please everybody.

Am I now trying to win the approval of men, or of God? Or am I trying to please men? If I were still trying to please men, I would not be a servant of Christ.
Galatians 1:10

~

140

There are no secrets to success. It is the result of preparation, hard work, learning from failure.

Sow for yourselves righteousness, reap the fruit of unfailing love, and break up your unplowed ground; for it is time to seek the Lord.
Hosea 10:12

≈

It is always easy to covet another man's success without envying his labors.

All hard work brings a profit, but mere talk leads only to poverty.
Proverbs 14:23

~

14

Try not to become a man of success but rather try to become a man of value.

Turn my heart to your decrees, and not to selfish gain.
Psalm 119:36
NRSV

~

Small numbers make no difference to God. There is nothing small if God is in it.

If you have faith as a mustard seed, you shall say to this mountain, "Move from here to there," and it shall move; and nothing shall be impossible to you.
Matthew 17:20
NASB

144

It is not enough to begin; continuance is necessary. Success depends upon staying power.

Be steadfast, immovable, always abounding in the work of the Lord, knowing that your labor is not in vain in the Lord.
1 Corinthians 15:58 NKJV

~

It is a deep-seated belief on the part of almost all Americans that their success will be better assured as they help to build the success of others.

Each of you should look not only to your own interests, but also to the interests of others.
Philippians 2:4

Success is to be measured not by wealth, power, or fame, but by the ratio between what a man is and what he might be.

The Lord judges the peoples; judge me, O Lord, according to my righteousness and according to the integrity that is in me.
Psalm 7:8 NRSV

The bridge between failure and success is hope.

Happy is he...
whose hope is in
the Lord his God.
Psalm 146:5
NKJV

Ⓗow you *define* success determines to a great extent whether you succeed.

Then Job answered the Lord, and said, I know that thou canst do every thing... So the Lord blessed the latter end of Job more than his beginning.
Job 42:1,2,12 KJV
~

To find his place and fill it is success for a man.

Desire that ye might be filled with the knowledge of his will in all wisdom and spiritual understanding; That ye might walk worthy of the Lord unto all pleasing, being fruitful in every good work.

Colossians 1:9-10

KJV

He has achieved success who has lived well, laughed often, and loved much.

I know the best thing we can do is to always enjoy life.
Ecclesiastes 3:12
CEV

And I can live my
life on earth
Contented to the end,
If but a few shall
know my worth
And proudly call me friend.

*Bear ye one
another's burdens,
and so fulfill the
law of Christ.
Galatians 6:2 KJV*

15

Wealth to us is not mere material for vainglory but an opportunity for achievement.

From everyone who has been given much shall much be required; and to whom they entrusted much, of him they will ask all the more.
Luke 12:48 NASB

Success is...seeking, knowing, loving and obeying God. If you seek, you will know; if you know, you will love; if you love, you will obey.

Grace and peace be multiplied unto you through the knowledge of God, and of Jesus our Lord, According as his divine power hath given unto us all things that pertain unto life and godliness, through the knowledge of him that hath called us to glory and virtue.
2 Peter 1:2-3

References

Unless otherwise indicated, all Scripture quotations are taken from the *Holy Bible, New International Version*® NIV®. Copyright © 1973, 1978, 1984 by International Bible Society. Used by permission of Zondervan Publishing House. All rights reserved.

Scripture quotations marked NKJV are taken from *The New King James Version* of the Bible. Copyright © 1979, 1980, 1982, 1994 by Thomas Nelson, Inc., Publishers. Used by permission.

Scripture quotations marked NASB are taken from the *New American Standard Bible*. Copyright © The Lockman Foundation 1960, 1962, 1963, 1968, 1971, 1972, 1973, 1975, 1977. Used by permission.

Scripture quotations marked KJV are taken from the *King James Version* of the Bible.

Verses marked TLB are taken from *The Living Bible*, copyright © 1971. Used by permission of Tyndale House Publishers, Inc., Wheaton, Illinois 60189. All rights reserved.

Verses marked NCV are scriptures quoted from *The Holy Bible, New Century Version*, copyright © 1987, 1988, 1991 by Word Publishing, Dallas, Texas 75039. Used by permission.

Scripture quotations marked NRSV are taken from The *New Revised Standard Version Bible*, copyright © 1989 by the Division of Christian Education of the Churches of Christ in the United States of America and is used by permission.

Scripture quotations marked CEV are taken from *The Contemporary English Version*, copyright © 1995 by the American Bible Society. All rights reserved.

Scripture quotations marked AMP are taken from *The Amplified Bible, Old Testament*, copyright © 1965, 1987 by Zondervan Corporation, Grand Rapids, Michigan. *New Testament* copyright © 1958, 1987 by The Lockman Foundation, La Habra, California. Used by permission.

Scripture quotations marked MLB are taken from *The Modern Language Bible, The New Berkeley Version* in Modern English. Copyright © 1923, 1945, 1959, 1969 by Zondervan Publishing House, Grand Rapids, Michigan.

Acknowledgments

Charles Colson (6), Booker T. Washington (7), Baron Pierre de Coubertin (8), Thomas Jefferson (9), Helen Keller (10), Grantland Rice (12), English Proverb (13), Charles Buxton (14), Logan Pearsall Smith (15), Vince Lombardi (16), Thomas Carlyle (17), Corrie ten Boom (19), H. M. Field (20), Norman Vincent Peale (21), Chapin (23), C. W. Wendte (24), Ron Dentinger (25), Harry J. Kaiser (26), Herschel Walker (27), Loretta Lynn (28), Huey P. Long (29), T. T. Munger (31), George Washington Carver (32), W. E. B. Du Bois (33), Carl Sandburg (35), Ben Azzai (36), An Wang (37), Bear Bryant (38), B. C. Forbes (39), Arthur Ashe (40), William Menninger (41), Henry P. Davison (42), Wofford B. Camp (43), Joseph French Johnson (44), Henry Ford (45,138), John Greenleaf Whittier (46), Homer (47), Charles "Tremendous" Jones (48,85), Dr. Frank Crane (49), Richard Brinsley Sheridan (50), Sammy Kershaw (51), A. T. Mercie (52), Charles Kendall Adams (53), Henry Ward Beecher (54,72,96), Joseph Addison (55), H. W. Arnold (56), Stewart E. White (57), Arthur Helps (58), Philip Chesterfield (59), Marie Dressler (60), Vesta M. Kelly (61), Bob Brown (62), Charles-Lewis de Secondat, Baron de Montesquieu (63), William J. H. Boetcker (64), John Stevenson (65), Denis Waitley and Reni Witt (66), O. Byron Cooper (67), Dolly Pardon (69) Pendar (71), Ann Landers (73), Thomas Fuller (74), Wilson Mizner (75), George Sand (76),

Theodore Roosevelt (77), C. Malesherbez (79), James Gordon Bennett (80), George F. Tilton (81), A. L. Williams (82), Leigh Mitchell Hodges (83), Jonathan Winters (84), Beverly Sills (86), E. H. Harriman (88), John Hayes Hammond (89), Eddie Cantor (90), William Shakespeare (91), Helen Hayes (92), Anna Pavlova (93), William A. Ward (97), Oswald Spengler (98), Henry Wadsworth Longfellow (100), Larry Bird (101), Joseph Heller (103), Marvin Feldman (104), Donald Riggs (107), Jackie Sherrill (108), Fancis Bacon (109), Albert Hubbard (110), David Frost (112), Abraham Lincoln (114), Sigmund Freud (115), Oral Roberts (117), C. S. Lewis (118), Charley Winner (119), Louis Pasteur (120), James Robertson (121), Oliver Goldsmith (124), Charles Evans Hughes (125), Margaret Thatcher (126), Miguel de Cervantes (127), Charles Rupert Stockard (128), John Wooden (129), Albert Einstein (131,143), Albert Schweitzer (132), Reggie Leach (133), Edward D. Simmons (134), David Gardner (136), Edward I. Koch (139), Herbert Bayard Swope (140), Colin L. Powell (141), D. L. Moody (144), J. R. Miller (145), Paul G. Hoffman (146), H. G. Wells (147), Phillips Brooks (150), Bessie A. Stanley (151), Edgar A. Guest (152), Thucydides (153), Charles Malik (154).

Dear Reader:

If you would like to share with us a couple of your favorite quotes or ideas on the subject of success, we'd love to hear from you. Our address is:

Honor Books
P.O. Box 55388, Dept. J.
Tulsa, Oklahoma 74155

Additional Copies of this book and other titles in the
God's Little Instruction Book series are available at your local bookstore.

God's Little Instruction Book
God's Little Instruction Book II
God's Little Instruction Book for Mom
God's Little Instruction Book for Dad
God's Little Instruction Book for Graduates
God's Little Instruction Book for Students
God's Little Instruction Book for Kids
God's Little Instruction Book for Couples
God's Little Instruction Book for Men
God's Little Instruction Book — Special Gift Edition
God's Little Instruction Book Daily Calendar
God's Little Instruction Book for Women

Tulsa, Oklahoma